JEFFREY S. AKERS

DIGITAL EVANGELISM

EXPANDING YOUR MINISTRY'S DIGITAL FOOTPRINT

THE DO'S AND DON'TS OF SOCIAL MEDIA IN THE CHURCH

Published by Love Works International
Edited by Dr. Kandy Morrell

Library of Congress Cataloging-in-Publications Data
Digital Evangelism, Expanding Your Ministry's Digital Footprint The Do's and Don'ts of Social Media in the Church / Jeffrey S. Akers

ISBN: 0-9705806-4-9 (ebook)
ISBN: 0-9705806-3-0 (print)

First Edition 2019
The BluPen, LLC trade printing Manufactured and Printed in the United States of America

Cover Design, Formatting and Layout by
Chelaé Cummings
www.theblupen.com

CONTENTS

ACKNOWLEDGMENTS

I give thanks to our Lord and Savior Jesus Christ and acknowledge that it is only by the grace of God that I have been fortunate enough to use my faith, gifts, and talents to help others in ministry and life. I'm most grateful for my mother, the late Carol Frances Akers, for her outpour of creativity, wisdom, support, and love and my Father Raymond F. Akers who continues to be the foundation of prayer that fuels my accomplishments. I have also been blessed over the years to have spiritual leaders that have deposited wisdom, knowledge, and strength into my life: the late Bishop Virgil Oats, the late Elder Alex Kitchen, Bishop John Tate Sr., and Suffragan Bishop Craig S. High.

The journey of digital evangelism would not be possible if it were not for the ongoing support of my good friend and brother, Mr. Darrell Brown. Thank you for your years of faithfulness.

Thank you to Mr. Dialo Moore and Mr. Darrell Riddick of Arche Designs for your work on the first Internet Church website. A special thank you to Dr. Kandy Morrell, my dearest friend and ministry partner, for her love and support. I pray this book will be a great tool and resource for all those who read it.

INTRODUCTION

Digital Evangelism is when someone uses the Internet and multimedia to spread the Gospel of Jesus Christ and the good news about a ministry and its mission. Digital Evangelism can be an awesome ministry tool for the 21st century when used properly. The Internet is unique in its ability to reach people. I believe it is a God-given tool for the whole church. Outreach websites designed with wise communication strategies, clear design, usability, and readable, enticing, jargon-free pages, will receive many visitors. Keeping a clean and simple look has proven successful within my decade of Digital Evangelism. It is very important that you don't believe that only large ministries with mega-sites can do web evangelism. Many spare-time web evangelists are working from home. You may be surprised to find that many of them are not technically gifted. Many opportunities do not require a lot of technical knowledge at all! I desire that these next several pages help equip you for effective Digital Evangelism.

1

DEFINE IT

Digital Evangelism and Social Media Ministry, is the process where a ministry, such as yours, can use the power of websites and social sites like Facebook, Instagram, Twitter to promote your ministry and organization. Because traffic from social media sites is usually highly targeted, the visitors are more likely to turn into supporters than those who find your website via a search engine query. Another important benefit of traffic from social media sites is that it is essentially free or relatively low cost compared to other forms of traffic generation.

However, social media marketing is a time consuming and very involved effort that is not appropriate for everyone. This form of ministry requires a good deal of involvement, both in terms of keeping up with all the latest trends and in maintaining ongoing relationships with potential followers. Social media invites a two-way conversation between the poster of the information and the reader. If the ministry owner ignores the second part of the equation, then the ministry effort is most likely doomed to fail. To execute a successful social media marketing campaign, the Ministry Media Team should review a list of components that define a successful campaign.

THE FIRST INTERNET CHURCH

I started Digital Evangelism with great enthusiasm thinking I would reach the world after I created my first ministry website, only to reach a few people in a couple of different countries. It was not the impact that I expected. But I knew God was leading me to continue. So, it was back to the drawing board for me. Then I began to dream of people learning about Christ while on their computers. I knew it was confirmation from the Holy Spirit. I began to research how to create a platform for the salvation message to reach more people. Then it suddenly became clearer than ever for me to build the world's first Internet Church. I started working on the concept in 1998. I was making progress but still not able to complete the vision. After all, social media had not been invented yet, but the frontier to communicate via the Internet was growing at an accelerated rate. New companies and ways to communicate were popping up everywhere. Companies and corporations were competing for something the average person was not aware existed. Many churches were just getting introduced to

WE ARE SAVED BY GRACE THROUGH FAITH. FAITH COMES BY HEARING.

the concept of a computer in the church. I shared my vision with several others. Most people just laughed and looked at me as if I was crazy. I was starting to wonder what it must have been like when Noah told others it was going to rain and built an ark.

I knew God had shared with me that this would be a way to expand the reach of the church. God kept me encouraged in spite of all the criticism and laughter from others. I had several people tell me that it was not a real church, and no one can get saved over the Internet. God reminded me we are saved by grace through faith and faith comes by hearing.

In 2013, with the help of a company called Pal-Talk, a video chat company that launched in 1998 now free to the public, I had my first interactive service online. It was amazing that me and my best friend and brother, who later would become a deacon for this ministry, were communicating and having a real-time church service via the Internet. I was in South Carolina, and he was in Michigan. Shortly after that, I sought the help of a web developer to integrate, build, and create an Internet church. The first 16 web developers told me it could not be done. The next five tried and could not get the coding to create the site. I was very discouraged at this point thinking to myself I've got one more web developer to talk to and if they can't do it, I'm done.

PEOPLE ARE MORE OPEN TO SHARING THEIR PROBLEMS VIA THE INTERNET.

With my funds depleted and my faith shaken, I took the meeting. I shared the vision with them. They were excited. They replied, "We have never tried anything like this, but we love a challenge." The company was Arche Designs, a small business startup owned by two guys passionate about what they did. They did not just build the site. They partnered with me because of faith and a vision. I was reminded of the scripture in Zechariah 4:10, "For who hath despised the day of small things? For they shall rejoice, and shall see the plummet in the hand of Zerubbabel with those seven; they are the eyes of the LORD, which run to and fro through the whole earth (KJV)."

After the completion of the web site, I knew it was much more than a website. It was, without doubt, a complete interactive ministry. In 2004, after a trip to the State Office in Columbia, South Carolina, I.A.C. World Ministries became an official Church with all the privileges and regulations like any other church. Our Internet Church also had all the same features as a physical church. It had a bishop, pastor, ushers, deacons, tithes and offering, and a choir. As an Internet pastor, I quickly learned people were more open to sharing their problems and needs via the Internet. By the third week, our prayer request button had generated over one thousand prayer requests. I was overwhelmed with trying to read them all but pleased with the response and progress.

TECHNOLOGICAL ADVANCEMENTS

By now, the Internet user base had almost doubled, and the first iPhone was launched. Social media was now picking up momentum all around the world after the 2005 launch of Facebook. The digital frontier of day to day communication was here to stay and growing so fast. Everyone just had to have an Internet presence. I was no longer alone. Many pastors and ministry leaders had caught the vision of Digital Evangelism. Everyone wanted a website for their church.

By 2014 most churches or ministries realized they needed some a presence within the digital community to be relevant. An Internet presence sounded great, but because most ministries did not understand the process, they were unsuccessful in many areas of Digital Evangelism. Many ministries today still do not have well-executed strategies or digital media practices. This book will serve as a guide to help your ministry get better results, amplify your ministry's message, and keep your church well informed. It can also be a great tool to win souls to Christ.

2

THE DO'S AND DON'TS

Message consistency is very important. Digital Evangelism requires consistency to build relationships with the recipients of the gospel. Please let me take this time to remind you this is a ministry and should be handled as such. Many people have become discouraged because they don't see any results from posting. There must be a consistent message to see results. Too many times, there are inconsistent postings by someone in the ministry sharing their opinions about other issues than the message of the ministry. To achieve consistency, you must take the time to write posts relevant to the ministry's message.

THERE MUST BE A CONSISTENT MESSAGE TO SEE RESULTS.

Those who want the truth will need more than just a one-time live stream or post. You can use Instant Messenger to connect with more followers when posting and live streaming. I also recommend that your ministry acquires an online phone number or another method of free communication. A Digital Evangelism team can help to achieve consistency, relevance, and effectiveness. I have had tremendous success in helping ministries build Digital Evangelism teams.

The basic team is made up of these volunteers in your ministry:

- Writer - good grammar skills and creative writing
- Altar Worker - one serious about soul winning
- Youth - likes posting and social media
- Tech - basic computer skills

The team will need training that will make your efforts more effective. We establish digital evangelism protocols for the team to follow. Learning and practicing the protocols increases cohesiveness among the team and the ministry. We make sure everyone is on the same page, with the same message, maintaining the ministry's brand, and following the Pastor's vision.

ESTABLISHING PROTOCOLS

THE ALTER IS PRIVATE!

These basic protocols protect the integrity of the ministry and the pastor from any legal damages. The altar is private, and many people do not wish to share this personal moment with the world. A sign can be placed in the sanctuary requesting people not post on social media of any format during altar call or baptism unless pre-approved by staff for insurance and legal purposes. Here are additional protocols that will be helpful and raise a respectable standard within your church:

- **PERSONAL OPINION.** Personal opinions can be considered Cyberbullying. Cyberbullying is a crime and can and will be treated as such under certain circumstances. It is important that you share what the Bible says about the subject matter and not your opinion.

ⓧ **The Wrong Way**

I don't care what you say men laying with men and women laying with women is a sin, and you are going to hell. You need Jesus. I stand for the truth.

✓ **The Right Way**

Stick to the Bible, never opinion.

God created humans to engage in sex only within the arrangement of marriage between a male and a female. (Genesis 1:27, 28; Leviticus 18:22; Proverbs 5:18, 19) The Bible condemns sexual activity that is not between a husband and wife, whether it is homosexual or heterosexual conduct.

- **STEALING DIGITAL REAL-ESTATE.** Not getting permission to post pictures flyers or videos on another person's site is considered rude and a breach of protocols. This type of rudeness is very common among the Christian community. Although you mean well, it is always the wrong thing to do without permission. The correct way is to inbox a person with a request.

The Right Way

Hey, friend, I have an upcoming event I would like to share on your page. Would that be okay? It would also be great if you would share it a well.

Many people have lost respect because those that are posting without consent did not show respect. There are protocols for Social Media and Digital Evangelism. Please make sure you and your ministry follow them. Failure to do so affects the complete movement of sharing God's word.

- **OVERKILL.** I know you are excited about what's going on at your ministry. Over-posting can repel viewers and supporters. Finding a balance is very important to the growth and development of your Digital Evangelism outreach program. Too many posts and too many people posting the same content leads to viewers not reading or responding to future posts. They might have viewed but are now turned off altogether because all they can see on their timeline is you over and over again. Too much posting can be worse than not enough. You should never post on your ministry site more than three times per day.

⊗ The Wrong Way

Post all day and tag your friends every hour. Share the post on everyone's timeline six times a day. Blast someone's inbox daily.

- **TAGGING, HASHTAGS.** If you're hosting a church service, special event, or regular worship service with a sermon series name, brainstorm and use a hashtag to engage your audience more effectively, hashtags can also help followers locate all posts relating to your ministry's event. When a follower pushes on the hashtag, all posts related to that hashtag are displayed. Followers can easily read information and views photos because posts are categorized within the hashtag.

✓ The Right Way

#empoweredforgreatnesss #LearnGreatness@iamchurch #Godslove@yourchurch

- **RESPONDING TO QUESTIONS PROMPTLY.** Not responding is unacceptable in any form of communication. But it is more noticeable in the digital age. When you are slow to respond or fail to reply altogether, you are leaving digital visitors with the impression that they do not matter to you, your ministry, or your church. Social media sites also rate your response activity and time with reward badges if you respond most of the time and quickly. These analytics are displayed for visitors to see. If your team responds quickly, it demonstrates that a more responsible, caring, party is attending to your site.

The Right Way

Answers messages immediately or within 24 hours of receipt.

- **MISTAKES HURT YOUR MINISTRY.** Too often ministries post misspelled words or content with the wrong date or time for a service. Some have used voice-to-text only to discover once it is too late that they have posted something inappropriate. In most instances, the inappropriate content is posted accidentally or is posted using a personal account. The administrator may post something he or she meant to send from a personal account or in a text, and instead of going to one or just a few people, it goes to several hundred or several thousand. Mistakenly posting to personal accounts is why it is necessary to have a separate account under the ministry name. Mistakes happen, but extra care is also needed. A small trained administrative staff can post to assure these situations do not occur. One administrator on every church account is needed.

The Wrong Way

Hop you can jon us for worship last Sunday at 3:00am with Pastor Hamburger

Following these basic digital evangelism protocols can help your ministry build respect, integrity, and a professional image and brand within social media. Your brand speaks for who you are and what you represent. As people of God, we represent Jesus. His excellence is never a protocol we intend to compromise. This standard will also help us build online relationships that could lead to soul winning.

SPECIAL NOTE TO PASTORS

Let me make this clear to pastors, ministers, and leaders. You may think you are not on the Internet because you do not have a social media site or Wi-Fi in your church, but you probably are. Many ministries are unaware of how, when, and what church members are posting. If what is shared of you as a speaker, preacher, or teacher is only shared in part, it could have a very negative impact on your ministry. Unapproved partial postings can be dangerous to your ministry. If the viewer is looking for answers and encouragement from the word of God but instead perceives a different message, ministries miss the opportunity to reach that person. Partial postings can also shape an untrue opinion of the ministry and the Pastor. Please make a mental note that many people viewing ministries online could be wanting, wounded, self-gratifying, or haters.

UNAPPROVED PARTIAL POSTINGS CAN BE DANGEROUS TO YOUR MINISTRY.

For those that fall in the wanting category, please be advised a great number of them have misleading intentions. They prey on pastors, ministries, and perhaps some of your church members. They start with a very compelling story of how they want JESUS. They will even ask you to pray for them. They will pull on your heartstrings with stories and photos that could influence you to give them what they want...money. You should always be in prayer and led by the Holy Spirit when ministering and communicating with anyone on social media.

Wounded people wander in hopes to find someone who cares so they can share their pain. Please understand this is a part of a ministry that is needed. Any wounded visitor on your site or live stream creates an opportunity for them to be healed. I strongly recommend that you not engage in ongoing conversations with them. God's word heals. Have the wisdom to give them the scriptures that give life. Many of the hurting already have a relationship with God. They have experienced church hurt, lost someone close, and are angry with God or the Church. The ministry of love and listening is all they need. Scriptures that affirm God's love is what they need. I want to remind you if you are working in this type of Digital Evangelism your responsibility is to minister, not trade stories of pain and process. Resist the urge to share your experiences. The focus must remain on God. He heals the broken-hearted. Some may even attach to your ministry. Be sure you are handling God's business instead of sharing yours.

Self-gratification is very common when it comes to social media and the modern church movement. When you share the Gospel, make sure your message is about the word of God, the works of God, and the Love of God. NOT ABOUT YOU!

It is also very important for all of your ministry staff and members to be reminded frequently not to engage in trying to correct or chastise those that appear to be false prophets. This is a trick of the enemy, and it will backfire on you almost every time. God did not call us to be his lawyer or his defendant. We must continue the message of love and hope. God's word shall stand. We must amplify it. The word of God reminds us that those that are false would come.

MATTHEW 7:15-17 (KJV)

15 Beware of false prophets, which come to you in sheep's clothing, but inwardly they are ravening wolves.

16 Ye shall know them by their fruits. Do men gather grapes of thorns or figs of thistles?

17 Even so, every good tree bringeth forth good fruit, but a corrupt tree bringeth forth evil fruit.

Don't be alarmed when you meet resistance in massive quantities. Satan will most certainly try to distract, intimidate, and slow you down. Digital Evangelism is a threat to satan and his followers. Let me put it in plain facts. There are currently 3.8 billion people that use the Internet. In the last ten years, there has been an increase in the number of people who believe in the Apostolic and Pentecostal doctrine like never before. How and why? Many countries now have access to preaching and teaching via the Internet.

Digital Evangelism is essential to the kingdom of God. The

word of God reminds us faith comes from hearing. We must spread the word by any means necessary. In just ten years, we have seen growth at an amazing rate. India now has 28 million Christian followers, which is 2.3 percent of India's total population. Pentecostalism has become a significant part of Latin America's religious and political landscape in recent years. According to 2005 figures from the World Christian Database, Pentecostals represent 13%, or about 75 million, of Latin America's population of nearly 560 million. In South Korea, a Pentecostal church is the largest megachurch in the world, with a congregation approaching 800,000 people.

Digital Evangelism is making an impact in spite of what you think or see. There will always be those that continue to hate and share a hate message. Thank God we now have a global platform to spread love, holiness, repentance, and the good news that JESUS is alive and saves. Be sure that you and your ministry stays focused on the mission of spreading God's word. Remember to preach and teach the Gospel consistently.

3

BUILD IT

Build relationships. As previously mentioned, establishing relationships with social media followers is one part of social media ministry that gives us so much power. We can build relationships by posting updates that users want to read about, such as ministry updates, new projects, and even your ministry or organizational history. We cannot post just a never-ending stream of funding requests.

> ***FORMING GOOD STRONG RELATIONSHIPS FOSTER ENDLESS POSSIBILITIES.***

You can open a two-way conversation with people via the comment sections and message boards that many social media sites have. You can also send invitations for people to like your page. When people like your page, your posts show up readily on their timeline, allowing you to reach them on a more consistent basis. If they like your posts, they also have the option to become a follower. The more followers you have, the more people you reach, the more people you reach, the more opportunities you have to build relationships that can turn into ministry opportunities. If people never see your posts, you are not effectively using the tool. A committed team will take the time to ask people to like and follow your page. If people like and follow your page, they might even share your posts, which increases your ability to reach more people, gain more followers, and build more relationships. These relationships can build credibility and help keep the ministry in the mind of the reader.

If you build relationships online, those relationships could result in people joining your Internet Church or attending your brick and mortar church. Forming good strong relationships foster endless possibilities. So, don't just view it as social media. View it as Digital Evangelism opportunities.

To be effective, we must maintain a consistent message. A social media manager or the hiring of a search engine optimization (SEO) services company is beneficial. When posting information across several different sites, it is easy for the message you are trying to convey to become confused as you try to tailor that message for a variety of media and audiences. The style we choose for Facebook will not work on Instagram, Gospel Tube, or Twitter, etc.

Many ministries or organizations do not have the experience or the time to learn the local lingo of all the various social media outlets. If you do not have the budget for an SEO services company, then it is best to limit yourself to the social media sites that you are comfortable writing for. You must also keep in mind many social media communities are rude, if not outright hostile to someone who shows up and has no interest in the site other than posting their promotional material. It is best to build a friendly following so that when you post, your message is welcomed and received. The more people who receive your message, the greater the impact your posts will have. For beginners, start with the social media platform that best compliments your style. Instagram posts are photo-based posts. If you love to post photos and don't want to write a lot of content, choose Instagram. If you like to engage with people more often, choose Facebook because it's centered more toward engaging conversations. Twitter is short phrases or sentences called tweets. What you write has a limited amount of characters or words. Whichever platform you choose, take time to use it, understand how it works, and become comfortable with it, so your posts have a greater impact.

4

PLAN IT. PROJECT 52

After serving as a Digital Pastor for over 16 years, I have refined a basic outline to help guide your ministry. This process, if followed and implemented correctly, can help you spread the Gospel and make a great impact on the world while enhancing your ministry objectives locally. The project goal is to pre-script 52 short posts: 52 different posts, 52 weeks of posting. The reason for pre-scripting is to ensure the same general message in many different ways is communicated to reach and educate people. Effective Digital Evangelism requires several steps. Understanding these steps are imperative to the success of your digital campaign.

MINISTRY AWARENESS

Ministry awareness requires more than just social media posting. This step is the foundation of your ministry, gaining momentum within the digital and social media sector. Ministry awareness requires creative writers that will write short paragraphs concerning ministry success and educational information. You also need those who are willing to work and research ministry history, accomplishments, and uplifting testimonies.

Be careful of what you post. In a rush to get new postings out the door, it is often tempting to skip editing, proofreading, and screening of the content. However, this is a very dangerous game. Unfiltered content has been the downfall of many ministries trying to establish a social media presence. Some ministries have even lost followers and supporters because they allowed someone to post their opinion.

The posts should all be created by a media team to ensure quality and consistency. Even a simple spelling error can turn an innocent post into a racial slur. So, it is imperative that your screen, edit, and proofread all content before posting it. This project will consist of posting sermons exhorts, class highlights, social media posts, and other information and testimonies that educate and inspire others to learn the necessary tools for spiritual growth, advancement, and successful living.

The formats for text posts should be an MS Word document (AP). An audio file should be MP3, 44 kilobytes, and be a snippet of 30 seconds to three minutes long. Video files are best formatted at as MP4 -720 or 1080P, 30 seconds to two minutes duration.

FILE MANAGEMENT

To accomplish effective Digital Evangelism, it takes strategic planning and good file management. Create an excel spreadsheet and add the name and address of each person reached that responds to your post from your email form, your website, or social media account. Encourage social media visitors to share their location. Why? The Mission is to reach and confirm 52 different States in the USA, 52 different cities, and 52 different countries.

To encourage participation, you should devote time in your Sunday service to help people engage on social media, which is one of the very things that can take the church outside of the four walls. During your welcome segment, ask people to take out their phones and tweet something or post something to their timeline. Ask them to share a picture or put some text up on the screen. Maybe you've already got time for shaking hands. Hugely expand that.

This method is also a way to invite people to your ministry via smartphone by posting regular, useful, or entertaining updates. The more often we share interesting or informative content with our followers, the more often we will catch their attention. To many, it may seem counterproductive to spend your time finding an article or blog post that your followers would like and then sharing it, but it builds credibility and authority in the eye of your digital visitors and participants.

Social media sites are usually tightly knit communities, particularly certain social media communities. The users of these sites can spot marketers a mile away, usually because the marketer does nothing more on the site than post information about various products. To gain trust and followers within one of these communities, you must be willing to participate as well. This is usually done in the form of commenting on the postings of others and the sharing or re-sharing of posts that have absolutely nothing to do with marketing or consumerism.

If you choose to hire an SEO services company, it will have a person or a team of people who are dedicated to maintaining community involvement on your ministry's behalf. Facebook is the leader for social media; this gives us the advantage to present new ministry information to the masses.

5

BLITZ IT

A blitz is an intensive campaign or attack. However, in the world of marketing, a blitz is used to describe a very short, intensive, and focused marketing campaign for a product, business, or organization. Our plan is simple: to utilize free social media and eblasts, to inform, to build relationships, and raise funds for the ministry. A well thought out plan and a team of volunteer workers ready to make a difference are needed.

Take into consideration that most of the required tasks take less than 30 minutes per week. Many tasks can be completed from a smartphone. All ministry media is also formatted to be smartphone friendly because smartphones and tablets are used more than desktop computers. Depending on the number of people who are subscribed to or follow your

GET YOUR MESSAGE OUT THERE TO AS MANY PEOPLE AS POSSIBLE!

pages, you have the opportunity to reach thousands in one blitz. Share and tag your posts to increase your potential reach.

SOCIAL MEDIA BLITZ

The goal is to get your message out there to as many people as possible within your target market. Creating posts that contain video, photos, flyers, or special interest announcements or stories centered around the campaign through social media accomplishes this goal. Your team should create a group of posts that help drive the campaign, incite interest, and call people to action. The campaign needs a beginning and an end, a central focus, and clear goals. The posts can be created and scheduled, so you don't have to manually. Using the scheduler function, you select the date you want your posts to play/post, and it will post for you at that time. This function will save time as you move forward with your campaign. If done strategically and properly, it will be beneficial.

PEOPLE NEED TO UNDERSTAND THE BENEFITS OF JOINING THE MOVEMENT!

Consider this. If the campaign is a membership campaign, the posts should be about the ministry, what it has to offer and explain the benefits of joining such a ministry. People need to understand the benefits of joining the movement to achieve buy-in for any campaign. Why should they join the movement? What is in it for them? How does it benefit them? When you answer these questions, you will be on your way to developing posts that people can engage in and possibly help accomplish your goal of increasing participation or membership. Many people fail at this stage because they don't take the time to think through the process. It is the same concept as when we present salvation to people. We explain to them the gospel of Jesus Christ, and then we explain what a new life in Christ looks like. We give them the benefits of salvation...forgiveness of sin, old things are passed away; all things become new, a new abundant life on earth and eternal life in heaven. People who understand those benefits and view them as valuable, receive it and are willing to accept the change. People who don't understand the benefits or don't understand there to be any benefits reject the change. You increase your chances of achieving buy-in for your cause if you present the benefits and help people to understand what you offer has value.

The social media platform, in many cases, has replaced print media advertising. I remember when a vast majority of our advertising was done using newspaper, yellow page phone books, and magazines. It was astronomically expensive. We spent $500-$600 a month with Yellow Page advertising, $10,000 a year with newspaper, and about $2,000 a year with a magazine and circular flyers. Now you can advertise on social media for free if you take the time to post, tag, and share. There are many free social media groups that you can share to as well that have strong followings and thousands of members, like classified ads and special interest groups. Taking the time to use social media to advertise your organization or products is well worth your time and saves you money.

EBLASTS

Eblasts are email campaigns that are used together with social media campaigns. These campaigns comprise the blitz. Email campaigns that include the same content as your social media posts can be created and sent to your website subscribers, church members, or any email database that you have built or purchased. It is important to collect email addresses every opportunity you get so you can build a strong database. This database enables you to connect with more people and keep them abreast of your events, appeals, and advancements. There are some free email marketing platforms that you can use like MailChimp. There are also some like Constant Contact that charge a small monthly fee to use their cloud-based software. These companies' software is easy to use. You can upload, drag, and drop, and customize your content as well as customize their free templates to build an eye-catching, effective email.

After your email is designed and created, you can send a test email to yourself or someone else on your team. A good review of the test email will help you see if any format or content changes are needed. When you are satisfied with the results, the email is scheduled to send to the database you select immediately, or if you choose, at a later time. This software will usually suggest when the best time to send is. They make suggestions based on their statistics of when people open their email, but you can choose any time that works best for you and your followers.

Once the email is sent, that is called blasting because you send an email to a complete database all at the same time. The software will provide analytics for you, like how many people opened your email, how many people clicked a link to your website, how many emails bounced back (returned because of a bad address or closed account), and how many new subscribers and unsubscribers. These analytics are helpful. You can determine which design, message, content, and overall email were most effective as well as who was interested in that particular content.

Some of the email marketing software will post to your social media at the same time the eblast is sent. However, I find that the look and feel of those generated posts are not as good as the ones you create specifically on the social media site. I suggest using the email marketing software exclusively for email marketing and then venture over to the social media sites and make those posts there.

SOCIAL MEDIA AD BOOSTING

After you have exhausted all the free advertising, the option for paid advertising is available. By boosting an ad (a post that includes a flyer, video, or photo), reaches more people. The ad is boosted or shown in the newsfeed of those people you target. This feature is easy to use by following the prompts and answering the questions. It helps to determine the demographics of the people you want to reach and then strategically is shown to the people you select. For instance, what is your target market? What age person, cities, states, gender do you want your ad shown to? How long and when do you want your ad displayed? How much money do you want to spend? What social media platforms do you want it shown? When these questions are answered, the algorithm displays how many people you can potentially reach. Your selections can be adjusted according to your advertising goals and should be realistically aligned, so your advertising dollars are well spent. If your ministry is boosting an ad to a local event, and the goal is to increase attendance, then boosting the ad to the local market makes the most sense.

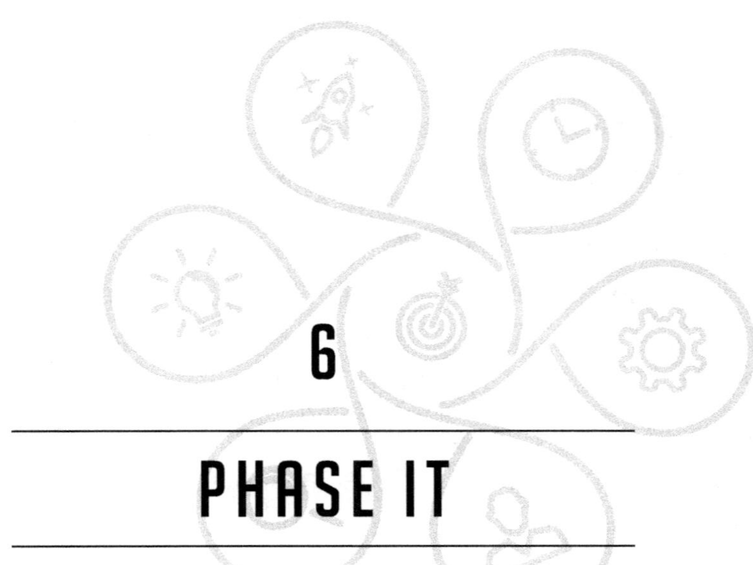

6

PHASE IT

PHASE 1: ESTABLISH THE TEAM

Recruiting multimedia team members to help build a digital ministry on social media networks is the objective in phase one. This team will create think tanks to produce content for all outgoing media post. The team will also create social media relationships by creating ministry accounts managed weekly by ministry media team members. Building an email-farm for a new database and outgoing email campaigns is also a task of the media team.

Ministry Media techs will be expected to make post updates once a week, check their designated media assignment frequently, and respond with only positive dialogue. Each team member that participates will be expected to follow specific guidelines while uploading posts. All posts are pre-scripted to ensure a consistent message with the ministry or organization.

The administration creates all passwords. Do not change the passwords at any time. This rule is important.

PHASE 2: TAGGING AND RATING

The team will create an Internet presence and social media followers. The team will also Metatag all sites and videos to make it more accessible and to locate your ministry online. Tagging will be a very vital part of your ministry, gaining momentum within social media and Internet presence. This task is not very difficult but does require a little more time. Blogs commonly use tagging; attach keyword descriptions (called tags) to identify images or text within their site as a category or topic. Web pages and blogs with identical tags can then be linked together, allowing users to search for similar or related content.

PHASE 3: VIDEO SHARING

Stage three deals with sharing your ministry's videos with followers and potential followers. This task is one that only requires updates quarterly and takes about fifteen minutes to complete. Create video updates of your ministry projects and progress. Upload ministry testimony videos quarterly to run effective media campaigns. To be effective, we require team members to select one video provider and manage it. To manage a channel, you must have a reasonably updated computer and high-speed Internet or smartphone. Your ministry will include a link to your website in the first line of each video description. Your ministry will release programming that appears on both media channels and ministry web site. For example, part one of a video is on your channel, but you can find part two on your site.

You will need to create a face for your ministry. YouTube is a community made of real people, and they want to see, hear, and interact with other real people. The connection to your organization becomes much more powerful if someone in your organization becomes the face of your brand. It changes the dynamic of the interaction from looking at videos from another company to building a relationship with a human.

Your ministry will also create a channel trailer that will only show up for non-subscribers. This method is a great way to introduce your channel and showcase your ministry brand in a fun and engaging way. At the end of the video, make sure to include a call to action asking the viewer to subscribe to your channel.

7

PERSONALIZE IT

Personalizing your media is a very important part of branding your ministry, the work, and the organization's leader. Consistency is also needed here. You can personalize your account with each digital media service provider. Many ministries or organizations don't take advantage of the opportunity because they don't meet the requirements. All icons are required to be a specific size. Please view the table below for sizes and dimensions needed for icons, headers, etc., so your ministry can personalize your media correctly.

SOCIAL MEDIA CHEAT SHEET			
FACEBOOK PAGE PHOTO SIZES	minimum	optimal	maximum
Cover Photo	400x150	1200x675	
Group Cover	n/a	1640x859	

SOCIAL MEDIA CHEAT SHEET			
Event Cover	n/a	1200x675	
Profile Picture	170x170	340x340	
Link Image	600x314	1200x628	1:91:1 ratio
Photo Post Widths for Quality	720	960, 2048	up to 2:3 ratio
Photo Viewer Max			2048x2048
PINTEREST PHOTO SIZES	**minimum**	**optimal**	**maximum**
Profile Photo	180x180	600x600	600x600
Pins (recommended)	600x600	600x900	600x1260
Board Cover	340x340	600x600	1:1 ratio
INSTAGRAM PHOTO SIZES	**minimum**	**optimal**	**maximum**
Profile Photo	110x110	180x180	crops round
Story Image		1080x1920	9:16 ratio
Photo Post	1080x566	1080x1080	1080x1350
TWITTER PHOTO SIZES	**minimum**	**optimal**	**maximum**
Header		1500x500	
Profile Photo	400x400	400x400	crops round
Tweeted Image	600x335	1200x675	any height
Twitter Card (link)	600x314	1200x628	1:91:1 ratio

SOCIAL MEDIA CHEAT SHEET			
LINKEDIN PHOTO SIZES	minimum	optimal	maximum
Profile Banner		1584x396	4:1 ratio
Profile Avatar		400x400	20,000
Update/blog post	600x314	1200x628	1.91:1 ratio
Company Cover	1192x220	1536x768	2MB
Company Logo	300x300	300x300	4MB
YOUTUBE PHOTO SIZES	minimum	optimal	maximum
Channel Art	1546x423	2560x1440	
Video Thumbnail	640x360	1280x720	
Channel Icon		800x800	

When you take the time to personalize your media, you brand it, so it is easily recognizable as a platform for your ministry. Personalizing also helps so not to be confused with ministries that have the same name and function. Your media will be identified as part of your brand. It is important also to make sure your posts demonstrate your ministry's goals. Therefore, your photos, graphics, and banners need to be professional because they are a reflection of you and your ministry. Taking time to review the photos before posting will be crucial because once you post it, the world can see it. Even though some posts can be deleted, people often have time to screenshot and share before you delete it. A thorough review of the photos, banners, flyers, and content will help minimize posts that don't reflect your image or brand. Settings and permissions can also help because it will require your review of every post before it posts. For instance, other people may tag or share posts to your page, but those posts cannot be seen unless you approve of the posting. The media will send you a notification requesting your permission to post to your page, giving you the option to approve or decline the posting.

INBOX/INSTANT MESSENGER

Instant Messenger and Inbox are features that can be used to send personalized messages to a group of people or individuals. The message goes directly to the intended person or group. This feature allows you to personally address the person you are speaking with, which may lead to an engaging conversation. These conversations could present a ministry opportunity, invitation to church or help develop a more personal dialogue between individuals or groups.

DIGITAL CANVASSING

Using the inbox or instant messenger feature to invite people to church can be considered digital canvassing, like going door to door, extending an invitation to a church event. You can send a message of greeting to open a conversation. If the person is available to chat, there is usually a green dot beside their name. If they want to engage in the conversation, they will respond. You can lead into a conversation the same way you would if you were in person standing at the person's door with a flyer in your hand. Identify yourself and who you represent. A warm greeting can be extended and then ask if you can share the invitation with them. The concept is the same as in-person canvassing and should follow your ministry's canvassing protocols. It's just digital. There is a real person at the other end of the chat, which may be a potential guest to your church or event. The chances of receiving consideration for the invitation increases because you are personally sending them the flyer or invitation rather than posting the flyer in the newsfeed because people who do not follow your page may not see it in the newsfeed. The newsfeed is like a running river of information that flows constantly. You have to catch as it goes by or maybe never see it again. If you send it to their inbox, it will stay there until they view it, similar to an email. If they have social media messaging on their phone, they can receive the message instantly depending on their settings. Instagram, Facebook, Twitter, and LinkedIn all have these features.

INTERNET MESSAGES ARE NEVER TRULY PRIVATE.

You can share the messages with others by clicking the share button inside the messaging platform. So, internet messages are never truly private although personalized, and should be considered public messages because of the ability to be made public quickly through sharing or using the screenshot feature and then sharing or posting to an open forum. When personalizing such messages, keep in mind the conversation has the potential to be public. The messages also remain in your inbox unless you delete it. This feature makes it easy to follow up on the people you invited to your ministry. You can review your messages and their responses to help you decide how you want to proceed when you canvas again. Be careful not to offend anyone during the canvassing process because like when going door to door, you can get the door slammed in your face, or cursed out! How it works on social media is, they can curse you out or block you, or report you. If they block you, you won't be permitted to contact them anymore. If they report you, the social developers review the conversation to see if you violate any of their community standards or rules. Some of the basic Facebook community standards rules address the following topics:

- Violence and Criminal Behavior
- Safety
- Objectionable Content
- Hate Speech
- Violent and Graphic Content
- Adult Nudity and Sexual Activity
- Sexual Solicitation
- Cruel and Insensitive
- Integrity and Authenticity
- Respecting Intellectual Property

Violation of any of these standards can result in account closure, which means you would have to wait several months before you could make another account and participate in their social media. The pendulum swings both ways. You can choose to block or report someone for the same reasons they can block you. During canvassing, I try to avoid conflict, remain friendly, and remember that I am Christ's ambassador and a representative of the ministry I pastor or attend.

GROUPS

Creating groups is a good way to personalize your social media presence as well. Your group name should be identifiable as a part of your ministry brand when you create a social media group. Choose a name that has your ministry name in it or one of your ministry tags. This branding enables your followers and friends to associate them with your ministry. Your friends and followers can be invited to join your group. Inside the group, you can share information or discuss topics relative to your ministry. Settings and permissions allow you to close the group to group members only or open the group to anyone interested in the posts. I typically like to close the group for members only. This way, only people who join the group can view the content. Closing the group also decreases the chance of people making rude or undesirable comments in your feed. Members of your group can become engaged as topics of interest are discussed. Group administrators can make posts, approve or deny memberships, and monitor posts to make certain the group abides by the ministry's protocols.

An advantage of groups is it lets you target a group of people who have common interests. People join the group because they are interested in the ministry, are connected to someone in the ministry, share the same cause, or just curious. Whatever the reason for joining the group, it presents yet another opportunity to minister. If your goal is evangelism, try to make sure you extend invitations to join the group beyond your ministry members. Otherwise, you are preaching to the choir or trying to evangelize people who don't need evangelism.

8

BROADCAST IT

Facebook and Periscope have platforms that allow its users to broadcast live videos. Broadcasting live using these two mediums is free and easy. You can broadcast using a cell phone, tablet, or computer. The possibilities are endless with broadcasting live. Telethons, talk shows, worship services, commercials, announcements, product sales, and the list goes on as to how broadcasting live can be used to help your ministry.

To have a greater impact when going live, I strongly recommend that you take advantage of the multimedia system that is already in place. It is very important that your live posting becomes a strategic event. Before going live, you should announce it on all other media platforms informing your friends and followers. These posts should explain who is speaking, the goals, and when the live stream will take place.

This formula will prove to be very successful even if you stream daily or weekly.

Many ministries and organizations go live every day and seem to have very little success. Let me first start by saying just because its free does not mean your ministry or organization is ready to go live. There are several different things that you should take into consideration. Is your organization's message conveyed in the visual live stream that you are broadcasting? For example, if you post on social media about love, faith, or advancement within the kingdom of God and you broadcast a live stream that is contrary to those values, then it is not functioning at a level of excellence. You have then done more damage than good. Allow me to make it plainer. If the praise team is not singing in key, the lighting is incorrect for broadcasting, others are talking during service, your audience is unresponsive, and the sound quality is poor, then these things need to be addressed before broadcasting live even if it is free. Millions of people around the world are viewing, and this may be your first and last time to reach them. Visually and audibly they should have a positive experience.

SUCCESS STRATEGIES

It is best to have a strategic plan when going live. For instance, if the plan is to broadcast live as a part of a fundraising campaign or to sell products, then you must have a link or button calling people to action. By pressing the link or button, people execute a donation or order a product. The strategy must ensure all pieces of the puzzle are in place before broadcasting, or you miss the opportunity to maximize the broadcast or reach your goal. If the plan is to gain exposure for the ministry, make sure you have the ministry's website or other tags in the post to effectively stay with your ministry branding. Hashtags are also good to reach people with the same interests because when a person clicks the hashtag, all posts with that same hashtag show up.

9

FUND IT

Most ministries and nonprofit organizations depend on charitable donations to help fund their cause. Sometimes this is challenging because they have to compete for donor dollars among other organizations that share the same cause. Often potential donors give because of their relationships and interest in the promoted cause. The problem many ministries have is not that their cause and work is not good but because not many people know about their efforts. Their circle of exposure is often small. When your work receives more exposure, awareness increases, people have an opportunity to resonate with your vision, partnerships can develop, and potential donors can contribute to your ministry.

POTENTIAL DONORS GIVE BECAUSE OF THEIR RELATIONSHIPS AND INTEREST.

Social media presents an excellent opportunity for ministries to promote their causes and ask for funding. Platforms like Facebook are committed to supporting nonprofit organizations. They developed Facebook fundraisers, which is a convenient way for charities to raise funds and for people to raise funds for their favorite charities. Charitable organizations that have 501c3 status from the federal government are qualified to raise money through Facebook fundraisers. When posts and live broadcasts are made using the organization's official Facebook page, they can create a fundraiser by adding a donate button. This button links to the organization's information populated from GuideStar, a company that has a listing of all government recognized nonprofit organizations. The information in GuideStar is used to tell Facebook's donations processing partner, Network for Good, where to mail the donations. So, it is important to have your organization's information updated in Guidestar. Updates can be made by visiting the Guidestar website. If not, your donations check could get mailed to the wrong address and take you months to get it to resent to the right location. No one likes to raise a lot of money for it gets lost in the mail!

Donations made using the Facebook Fundraiser tool do not incur processing fees. Facebook generously assumes all processing fees for charitable organizations using this tool. If your organization does not have 501c3 status, you can still ask for donations via Facebook by adding a link to your organization's website. The link you post should take contributors to the donations page on your website. There they can process their donation. Processing fees apply to these donations according to the terms and agreement you have set up in your website with processing companies like Paypal or Square.

CREATE A CAMPAIGN

Fundraising campaigns are strategic plans that help you focus your fundraising efforts and maximize your chances for success. To develop a fundraising campaign, you need a catchy title that describes your effort. Next, you need media like video and photos to help show people the cause and reason why you need funding. You then need stories or posts that people can resonate with. These stories and posts should tell people about the cause, how many people you are serving, why you are passionate about it, the benefits to the donor, and the impact their donation will make. Finally, you need a fundraising goal.

Here is an example of a campaign we created. It was entitled, A Million for Missions. This campaign's social media portion launched with a professional video showing missions work, the organizational leaders, the goal, the level of giving requested which was $1/day or $365, and the ways to give like the website address, mailing address, and social media handles.

We posted weekly updates to our followers and contributors. Our team tagged and shared the posts with people within the organization. They tagged and shared it with their friends and followers. We boosted a few of the posts by paying for Facebook to show it to our target market, which increased our exposure. We made sure each post contained our hashtags, website address, and a Facebook donation button. One person within the organization raised $3,000 for the organization in just two weeks using this method because people can create fundraisers to raise money for their favorite charity the same way charities can raise money for themselves. Once people started seeing our campaign, momentum grew, and it went from being a campaign to a movement. More people wanted to support our cause, became engaged, and helped us raise funds. We raised approximately 700,000 in four years with this campaign. Sound amazing? It was. This result is what the favor of God, a good strategy, and a fundable cause can get you. You can use the same concept in your ministry. You will need to customize it to meet your needs, though.

ONCE PEOPLE STARTED SEEING OUR CAMPAIGN, MOMENTUM GREW, AND IT WENT FROM BEING A CAMPAIGN TO A MOVEMENT.

SETUP INSTRUCTIONS

- Open Create a Post on Your Facebook Page
- Look at the Icons Below. Click Support Nonprofit
- In the Search Bar Type the Name of the Charity You

Want to Support

- Click on The Charity's Name
- Write an Engaging Post Telling People Why You Want Their Support
- Post the Story
- Set Your Fundraising Goal by Entering the Dollar Amount
- Set a Start and End Date in the Designated Fields
- Invite Your Friends and Followers by Clicking Invite Friends
- Make a Donation to Drive Traffic to Your Fundraiser
- Make Weekly Updates by Posting Stories and Photos
- Send a Thank You Post to Your Contributors When They Give

GIVING TUESDAY

Let's take another look at how Facebook fundraisers can help your ministry. #GivingTuesday, a global giving movement was designed to help nonprofit organizations raise funds around the holidays. #GivingTuesday is the Tuesday after Thanksgiving. It falls in line behind Black Friday, Small Business Saturday and Cyber Monday. Next comes #GivingTuesday. There is a big social media push on Giving Tuesday (#GivingTuesday).

Each year Facebook partners with a large foundation to match millions of dollars of donations on that day. Last year, they partnered with Paypal and gave away 7 million dollars within seconds after the matching window opened.

Facebook fundraisers brought in 125 million for charities on #GivingTuesday. How it works: Individuals create Facebook fundraisers from their personal pages to raise funds for their favorite charities. The matching opens at 8:00 am EST. The first people to get their donations posted have a chance to be matched 1:1 by Facebook. It is first come first serve. One of the organizations I helped create a campaign for raised over $22,000 that day. Another one was matched $2,500 by Facebook for their organization, which means they raised $2,500 from friends and followers through their Facebook page, and Facebook gave them $2,500. The key to receiving a match from Facebook is the early bird gets the worm. All of the Facebook matching funds were depleted before 8:01 am EST. You have to have your donors ready to press that donate button right at 8:00 am to have a chance at receiving a match. After the matching is over, you can still raise funds all that day by encouraging your friends and followers to remember your organization on #GivingTuesday.

Many campaigns continue for a week after #GivingTuesday giving latecomers a chance to give. You can also partner with other organizations who want to support you by asking them to match you on the funds your organization raises on #Giving

Tuesday. Many charities have other corporate matches and have raised large sums of money to help their cause. Sometimes it is just making the right connections, being brave enough to ask, and knowing how to get the job done. #GivingTuesday is in its eighth year. I just found out about it two years ago. We have participated in #GivingTuesday ever since, and it has been a blessing to our nonprofit and the ones I market. Once we know about an opportunity, we cannot allow it to pass us. You can find out more about #GivingTuesday and get free campaign tools by visiting their website wwwgivingtuesday.org.

ONCE WE KNOW ABOUT AN OPPORTUNITY, WE CANNOT ALLOW IT TO PASS US!

YOUTUBE DOLLARS

If you have a Youtube channel and upload your videos, you could earn money depending on how many views your videos get. Advertisers pay between .10 to .30, an average of .18 per view. This means you could be paid about $18 per 1,000 ad views. This is why people love it when their videos go viral because it increases the chances people will click on ads displayed during their video, and then advertisers will pay them. Of course, this only works if the person views or clicks on the ad. Studies show that many young people watch Youtube videos more than they watch television. So, if your goal is to reach a younger audience, Youtube might be a great place for your promotions.

GET STARTED

Whatever medium you use in addition to your website can enhance your fundraising. People love convenience. Using social media makes it easy for people to give from any place at any time to help you meet your goals. Begin thinking about expanding your reach. There is a world of people out there waiting to learn about your work. They could be your next contributor. The Bible says we have not because we ask not. It doesn't take a lot of people. Sometimes it only takes the right person at the right time to help you reach your fundraising goal. Remember when people take ownership, they can become partners and stakeholders in your ministry. They can become friends and followers that are passionate about your cause.

10

PROTECT IT

The Internet is known to be a place where people can exercise their freedom of speech. However, when you share your opinion as a representative of your ministry or organization, it becomes an official statement representing your ministry. Any words that are not scripture-based can be damaging to certain parties, and in some cases, legal action can be taken against a ministry or its representatives. Therefore, developing a Social Media Policy is essential for any ministry. This policy gives guidelines for your social media team to follow. Without a policy, people might make offensive posts against the desires of the ministry's leadership. These types of actions can also put the ministry at risk of legal suits. You want to make sure your team and

DEVELOPING A SOCIAL MEDIA POLICY IS ESSENTIAL FOR ANY MINISTRY.

the ministry is using social media to shed a good light on the ministry and represent as God's ambassadors. Each member of the social media team needs to sign the policy acknowledging having read it and are agreeing to abide by the policy. You also want to make sure your ministry's insurance policy includes a rider that covers Internet activity. In most states, people can sue anybody for anything. Insurance coverage and adherence to policies add a layer of protection for you and your ministry. Here are the components of a good social media policy and can be used as a template for your ministry.

SOCIAL MEDIA POLICY TEMPLATE

This policy is to be used and adhered to by ministry leaders, employees, pastors, and volunteers of XYZ church/organization. This policy stands as the precedent of this ministry and conveys the desires of the ministry leadership. Any person using social media in connection with this ministry is to follow the set policy.

- **TAKE CARE.** Take care in posting the right message to the right platform. Post messages that are for ministry members in the group forums. Post evangelical messages in the open forums.

- **BE CAREFUL.** Be careful not to post private or sensitive information on the Internet. Understand that social media, blogs, chats, Instagram photos, screenshots, inbox messages, text, or multi-media messages in any form are Internet-based. These messages are considered public because they have the potential to become public quickly. Understand that once it is "out there," we cannot get it back. Before you post anything on social media, think of potential legal ramifications and consequences. The harvesting of past social media communications is now a common way for legal teams to find incriminating statements which can be used against you in a court of law. Employers often peruse social media accounts also of their employees. Many employees have been fired because of the content they posted on social media.

- **BE WISE.** Be wise so as not to get caught up in debates or arguments on social media. If disagreements ensue, speak about it in person as the Bible instructs, remembering not to air dirty laundry on the Internet for the world to see. We must have a spirit of unity, love, and evangelism. He who wins souls is wise as a serpent and harmless as a dove.

- **GO, TEAM.** Team members work together to advance the kingdom using social media. If you are not an authorized team member, do not make posts that represent the ministry. Seek approval first and join the team if you want to represent our brand.

- **DO RIGHT.** Team members who refuse to follow the ministry's social media protocols, break the social media's platform standards, make illegal actions, or perform any activity that embarrasses the ministry or blemishes its brand will be sanctioned or removed from the team.

- **GET PERMISSION.** Get permission in person, via text, email, or inbox before posting images or video of people obtained during a worship service, closed activity, or sensitive event that could expose a person's privacy or intimacy in worship. Don't post prayer requests associated with peoples' names. Take into consideration that not everyone wants to be blasted on the Internet.

- **DON'T PLAGIARIZE.** Don't copy and paste other people's writings, videos, photos, music, images, or graphic designs into your posts or creations as if they are your own. If you use someone else's material, you must give them proper credit for it and obtain written permission. Plagiarism is the same as stealing. Permission can be obtained from the owner of the content or via licenses that the ministry can acquire.

- **REPORT IT.** Report it to the ministry leadership or social media team leader if you see any content that goes against the ministry's standards, policies, or brand. Reporting will enable the ministry to take action for correction.

- **STAY ADULT.** Social media posts are geared towards an adult audience. Don't engage with minors on social media. Should a minor make contact, direct them to have their parents contact us. Team members who have engaging conversations via social media with minors violate our protocols and open the door to other possible problems. There are social sites designed for minors, and that is not where we are. Don't post photos or information about minors without their parents' consent, doing so could expose minors to predators or others trying to contact minors without parental consent.

- **MONITOR ALL.** Monitor all postings and tagging concerning the ministry. Monitoring should be done daily to secure quality and be aware of any problems. There should be at least two people that monitor it regularly. Monitors can be administrative staff outside of the media team to assure the safety, objectivity, and consistency. If something is found that is against our standards, delete it immediately. If the content is offensive, take provisions to block the person from our pages without explanation.

- **STAY BRANDED.** Remember all posts, videos, flyers, photos, and content must stay within our branding using our official name, logo, colors, address, phone numbers, and leadership names. Delete posts that do not stay within our branding.

- **GET INSURED.** Make sure the insurance policy contains a rider that covers the ministry and its employees, volunteers, and leadership for social media and Internet activity liability.

- **SIGN AND SEAL.** Every member of the social media team must sign and accept the social media policy. Their signature states they have read and accepted the policy. Members must complete a training class before they begin working with the team.

The social media team is a ministry of the church/organization. Each member agrees to follow the protocols and act Godly when engaging on any social media platform. By signing this policy, I agree to abide by the guidelines therein, accept the terms of the policy, and live within the standards of the church/organization. I understand further that my personal social media presence is not subject to these terms, but I do understand that it may influence the image of the ministry. I will, therefore, take care of what I post as I am a representative of Christ and this organization.

Team Member ______________________ Date______

Team Leader Verification ______________ Date______

***Note: This is a template. Your organization is responsible for compliance with all applicable laws. Accordingly, this sample should not be used or adopted by your organization without first being reviewed extensively and approved by an attorney. We assume no liability in connection with the use or distribution of this template. ***

People who do not have policies and guidelines to follow, typically make up their own rules as they go along. This kind of behavior can cause damage and undo the hard work you have put in to establish your brand, image, and reputation. Training permits you to take a proactive approach and ensure quality within your ministry.

11

IMPACT IT

The impact our Digital Evangelism efforts have made over the years has been tremendous. Through I.A.C, our Internet church, we have baptized several people in the name of Jesus. We have referred several people to other ministries in several cities and countries. One of our Internet members who lived in Michigan wanted baptized. So, I flew to Michigan and baptized the person. Several people have been healed and led to Christ.

The Internet church has also had revivals and several different speakers over the years, and many people receive online video counseling.

Some of the worst things that have happened in Digital Evangelism is I have had several virtual attacks and viruses trying to shut us down. I have had personal death threats. Almost every month for the past 16 years, someone comes online and tries to disturb or distract the service. I have been cursed out with some of the vilest and wicked words. I have heard some online pastors have been stoned for preaching the Gospel. Another pastor that was a part of our Internet church for several years had his house burned down, computer destroyed and had to flee with his family for his life.

I think the most impact for me as an Internet pastor was two things; my Bishop was a faithful and supportive member, and one summer I learned that the Internet services preaching were being broadcasted to an African refugee camp of forty thousand people for four weeks straight. We may never know all of the ways God will use us through Digital Evangelism, but we know the word of God is going out and making a great impact.

12

EVANGELIZE IT

After reading this book, I hope you are excited about Digital Evangelism and the opportunities available to share the Gospel via the Internet. Digital evangelism is an extremely powerful tool to share JESUS with people in hard to reach places and countries that don't allow Christianity. Many of the people that are looking for spiritual direction look online hoping to find the truth. Where we may have been limited to our local communities, now we can go global. The whole world can now be our evangelism field. With this in mind, I have compiled some tips to help you with Digital Evangelism.

HELPFUL TIPS

- Be Consistent and Available.
- Make it easy for people to find you on search engines.

- Keep URLs simple and always post how people can tune in.
- Prayer plays a big part of digital evangelism.
- Be sure to assess the needs of those who participate in your digital evangelism.
- Be sure to invite them to read the Bible.
- Share your testimony virtually. It is important for you to be able to write out your story—not to memorize and share it verbatim, but because it helps to put into words some of the important and interesting details of your conversion.
- Always leave a Bible verse and thought.
- Stay connected to your virtual audience with newsletters, posts, and emails to help keep them encouraged.
- Help them find a Church home in their area or close by that teaches and believes the truth and love of Christ.
- Remember it's not all about you or your ministry but rather the Kingdom of God.
- Provide your digital audience with links that keep them connected to the word, not just you.

- Choose video or audio snippets that support the teachings of Christ. The more they learn, the more influence your ministry has to help them find their way to truth and relationship with God.

AFTER CARE AND DIGITAL DATA

Aftercare ministries are very important. Many churches and ministries take the time to create visitor packages for those who visit the church. This practice has proven to be successful when implemented correctly. The process that works for the brick and mortar ministry can be effective with those who visit your ministry's social media pages, websites, or blogs. Taking time to follow up with a simple digital card that says thanks for visiting or we care can connect with those who view or visit your ministry site. People are always accepting when you show you care.

Social media and websites with free registration launch pages help provide analytics for you free of charge. Analytics is a powerful tool for evangelism. The analysis could show you how often a visitor views the page, what they liked on the page if they shared it with a friend, and with who they shared it. When you learn what area your visitors need help in, you can provide more content to lead them to Christ, more effectively build relationships, extend a personal invitation to your ministry, and invite more friends, who can learn about your ministry and what you offer the community. Also, you can expand the ministry's digital footprint.

CONCLUSION

Change is evident. The world and its system are rapidly changing. Leaders who want to stay relevant in this time must seek to go global using the Internet platforms available to help us reach the lost and minister to the hurting. Technology has changed some of the methods and procedures we use to evangelize, but our message of hope and healing is the same. Jesus is still the answer for the world today. We must remain consistent with our message. People depend on us to take the Gospel of Jesus Christ to the world. We can do it. We must do it. We must evangelize. Digital Evangelism is a tool that helps us spread the good news that Jesus saves. Let us use it and use it wisely to win the world for Christ.

ABOUT THE AUTHOR

JEFFREY S. AKERS is the founder and senior pastor of I Am Church, Greenville, South Carolina, and of the first Internet Church in the nation, I.A.C. World Ministries. He is also an international evangelist, certified life coach, multi-media director, assistant overseer, and international mission expert with missionary works in India and Jamaica.

Akers' passion for spreading the gospel through film and television is demonstrated in his work as founder of Inner-City Gospel, a gospel music talk show which has aired on numerous networks and streamed online for more than a decade and as a filmmaker in his company, Jeff Akers Films. Two of his recent film productions, *Homeless in the South*, a documentary, and the sci-fi Christian film *Illumination*, have garnered more than nine awards including Best Film Scoring, Best Actors, and Best Costumes. In addition, he has developed many social media marketing campaigns that have collectively helped raise millions of dollars in corporate America.

His wealth of experience, passion for change, and love for God and people drives him to minister to the hurting, aid the less fortunate, and empower people for success.

To learn more about Akers' vision, visit **www.jeffakers.net.**